FIRST BLUES

Rags, Ballads
& Harmonium Songs
1971-74

Allen Ginsberg

Full Court Press

ACKNOWLEDGMENTS: A few of these words for music've been published by Nuspeak Feature of Scottish Arts Council (Glasgow), Scottish International, Berkeley Barb, Phoenix Bookshop, Cross Country, "the", Chicago Review, New Age Journal, Choice, Earth Magazine, Peace and Pieces, Garage Sale, Six Pack, Pomegranite Press, Intrepid, Fervent Valley, Loka, Gay Sunshine/ Fag Rag, San Diego Door, Unmuzzled Ox, U of KC Student Newspaper: Spit in the Ocean, Bountiful Lord's Delivery Service (Lama Foundation).

Library of Congress Cataloging in Publication Data

Ginsberg, Allen, 1926-
   First blues: rags, ballads & harmonium songs, 1971-74

   I. Title
PS3513.I74F5   784   75-23082

ISBN   0-916190-04-8   (cloth)
ISBN   0-916190-05-6   (paper)

Full Court Press, Inc.
249 Bleecker Street
New York, New York 10014

Music notation is by Arthur Russell except for *Guru Blues*, which is by Allen Ginsberg.

Dedication
To Minstrel Guruji Bob Dylan

EXPLANATION OF FIRST BLUES

Although I studied Piano & Violin unsuccessfully a year in the 'thirties, and sang in bathrooms and on bridges solitary in the next decades, I did not begin chanting until visit to India and Japan in 1963, where impressed by Prajnaparamita Sutra & Hare Krishna Mantra, I borrowed Peter Orlovsky's tiny Benares Harmonium and began singing these magic formulae in invariable C chord. I practiced that monochordal mantrachanting all through the 'sixties at poetry readings, explaining that it was related to Poetry in measuring the breath through vocalization. Robert Duncan reminded me at Vancouver poetry conference 1963 that I used my body's inspiration more deeply in chanting Hare Krishna than I did in reciting my poetry.

In 1968 returning up Bayshore Highway on bus from visiting Neal Cassidy's household and touching silken bag of his ashes, I kept hearing musical fragments of Blake's *Grey Monk* moaning through my brain, and other fragments of Blake, including

> Fayette, Fayette, thou'rt bought & sold,
> And sold is the happy morrow
> Thou gavest the tears of Pity away
> In exchange for the tears of sorrow.

I experimented improvising music in F chord to the *Grey Monk* on a Uher tape machine given me as Christmas present 1965 San Francisco by Bob Dylan, who suggested that I learn an instrument and sang the *Grey Monk*

> But vain the Sword & vain the Bow,
> They never can work War's overthrow.

in Lincoln Park Chicago at political Convention time over microphone summer 1968, & sang it alone under a tree in the park to Phil Ochs, devout folk-singer. Police state shock despair experienced after kidnapping by Secret Service & frustration of peace protest marches opened me to the immediate poignance of Blake's songs, their prophetic simplicity, so returning to upstate NY gas-lit farmhouse I stayed up several nights pumping chords on an antique organ, improvising on tape tunes for the bulk of *Songs of Innocence & of Experience*—the inspiration for setting Blake's words, syllable by syllable according to vocal tones appropriate to their meaning, led me, by the time I reached Innocence's *Chimney Sweeper*, to discover a second chord, moving from C to F. I completed & recorded 22 of the songs using only 2 chords in 1969,[1] accompanied by helpful genius musicians including Jon Sholle, Don Cherry, Elvin Jones & Bob Dorough. Soon after that, street musician Gary Getz suggested that I adapt last lines of songs like *Spring* and *Nurses Song* to mantric refrain, repeated indefinitely long time as chorus with friend audience.

In San Francisco summer 1971 I recorded another album-length set of Blake songs, adding a few country-western changes suggested by Jon Sholle, I met Chogyam Trungpa, Tibetan Buddhist meditation teacher, whom I'd known briefly in the East. When I mentioned that I was fatigued by cross-country poetry readings he replied, "That's because you don't like your poetry." I said "What?" and he continued, "Why depend on a piece of paper when you recite poetry, don't you have your own mind, do like the great poets, like Mila-Repa, improvise spontaneously on the spot!" It was the same challenge that Kerouac had offered decades before, spontaneous mind-mouth tongue. I shaved my beard and began that night, improvising a stupid smart ditty rhyming June Moon and Beer Dear at his prompting after his dharma discourse. And the next night in Berkeley at benefit for N'yingma Meditation Center, got onstage with chorus and chanted over an hour with Harmonium Om Ah Hum Vajra Guru Padma Sidahi Hum and then with 2 chords did improvise a twenty minute lament, "How sweet to be born here in America..."

That Fall in NY Peter Orlovsky and I gave poetry reading at NYU in Greenwich Village, and improvised for an hour on the theme "Why write poetry down on paper when you have to cut down trees to make poetry books?" following a thought Gregory Corso'd writ, "No good news can be written on bad news." Unbeknownst to us Bob Dylan was in the audience, in the rear with old musician fellow-actor companion Dave Amram. Dylan phoned that night and asked, "Can you make up words like that anytime?" and came over Lower East Side apartment, picked up guitar, played various blues chords and latin rhythms & I sat on edge of bed and tongued syllables & sentences rhymed fast as I could to "I'm going down to Puerto Rico." So Dylan pleased by this proficiency said "Why dont we go into a studio and record?"

The first songs in this book are products of those sessions November 17 & 20 1971, and *September on Jessore Road (Fall of America)* was written between sessions to offer Dylan a text equal to his own genius and sympathy. Songs were written in studio while musicians waited, run over once, and recorded, choruses and breaks arranged much by Dylan. *Many Loves* and *Jimmie Berman Rag*, were improvised accidentally, in one take, and I've left texts awkward untouched.

I started going to folk music concerts, Happy Traum had played with us in studio, at one of his concerts in Peace Church N.Y. December 20 I got inspired to imitate common song style & wrote words for *NY Blues* and *NY Youth Call Annunciation* in pocket notebook in my pew, listening to his Woodstock folk band. In the last month Dylan and others had explained the use of third chord (14151—C F G—I still hadn't mastered that transition during the recording sessions, confusing musicians with my insistence that Jessore Road was a Blues)— and so I set out composing traditional twelve bar blues by Christmas

>Radiator Cockroach
>>Waving your horns at the wall
>What'll I feed you
>>I don't eat meat at all
>Go tell the bedbug
>>He better stay out in the hall

iii

By this time I had picked up a copy of Sackheim's[2] breath-stop-arranged transcriptions of classic blues, and was modeling my first blues on Richard Rabbit Brown's *James Alley Blues,* heard on Harry Smith's collection of American Folk Songs[3].

Sam Charters scholar reminded me that old blues & calypso were a vehicle for low down funky sex thoughts (& politics), "I got nipples on my titties as big as your thumb" was that Ma Rainey singing? I'd listened to blues Paterson N.J. high school days over WNYC radio—heard Leadbelly program live for a year, *Irene* & later *Black Girl* haunted me like Eli Eli—and hear Ma Rainey's *CC Rider* & *Jellybean Blues,* Bessie Smith's *Empty Bed, Baby Doll* & *Christmas Blues,* & later with Kerouac and Huncke in 'forties heard Billie Holiday's *Fine & Mellow* & *Hush Now Dont Explain*—and I'd sung ragged ditties & tocattas & fugues with Kerouac under Brooklyn Bridge in 1945–49 and listened with him and Neal Cassady to car radio Rhythm and Blues of Louis Jordan & Fats Domino & moans of Slim Gaillard & shrieks of Little Richard, so I had some kind of American Blues in my heart without knowing it—I could sing but didnt reckon it important poetically, until I met Krishna & remembered Ezra Pound's ken that poetry & music, song & chant (and dance) went together before the invention of the printing press and long after—forgotten by the same academies that forgot that the genre of American Black Blues & rags was as great a treasury of poetics as Bishop Percy's *Reliques* & Scottish Border Ballads & Elizabethan song books & Tom 'O Bedlam folk treasuries.

In the course of working with adept musicians for recording to fix Blake tunes for future generations I began to notate melodies crudely, developing child-simple lead sheets handy & workable for fast pick-up of the melodies—a sample of that's given in notation of the last song *Guru Blues.* As most of the earlier songs were developed in improvisation & practice before poetry audiences without lead sheets, the bulk of the music was notated by Buddhist pop star Arthur Russell who taught me new chords & played cello on Blake & later Dylan recording sessions.

The doggerel element in the poetry has to be dealt with—perceptive doggerel inexcusable & inevitable in the process of learning to sing and making up words on the spot. The ideal as in Campion & Nashe is a series of swift images, Dylan's "Chains of flashing images." Music carries senseless vowels, which could be revised but in keeping with the spirit of this Art I've left most first drafts & improvisations fixed in their original wordings, useful to myself & others to see how raw mind actually sings.

1. *Songs of Innocence and of Experience Tuned by Allen Ginsberg*, M.G.M., N.Y., 1969, Verve/Forecast FTS3083, reissued M.G.M., 1974.
2. Eric Sackheim, *The Blues Line*, New York, Grossman, 1969.
3. *American Folk Songs*, vols. I and II, New York, Folkways Records, 1952.

Allen Ginsberg
Kerouac School of Disembodied Poetics
Naropa Institute, Boulder, Colorado
June 30, 1975

CONTENTS

*Music notation included

FIRST BLUES

VOMIT EXPRESS

I'm going down to Puerto Rico
I'm going down on the midnite plane
I'm going down on the Vomit Express
I'm going down with my suitcase pain

You can take an ancient vacation
Fly over Florida's blue end
Rise up out of this madhouse nation
I'm going down with my oldest tender friend
                    I'm going down, etc.

We know each other now 20 years
Seen murders and we wept tears
Now we're goina take ourselves a little bit of Free Time
Wandering round southern Poverty Clime

Start flyin with those poor old sick ladies
Everybody in plane crowded & drunk & they're crazy
Flying home to die in the wobbly air
All night long they wanted the cheapest fare

Land there dawn on the airfield I never been there
Except once walking around on the airfield in the great wet heat
Walk out & smell that old mother lode of shit from the tropics
Stomach growl Love O friends beware—

Me & my friend no we won't even drink
& I won't eat meat I won't fuck around
Gonna walk the streets alone cars all blink & wink
Taxi buses & U.S. gas all around

Start with poetry at the University meet kids
Look at their breasts touch their hands kiss their heads
Sing from the heart maybe the Four Buddhist Noble Truths
Existence is suffering, it ends when you're dead

1

Go out & walk up on the mountain see the green rain
Imagine that forest vines get lost
Sit crosslegged meditate on old love pain
Watch every old love turn to ghost

See raindrops in the jungle Rainbows ants & men
Brown legs walk around on mud roads
Far from U.S. Smog War again
Sit down Empty Mind vomit my holy load

Come back to earth, walk streets in shock
Smoke some grass & eat some cock
Kiss the mouth of the sweetest boy I can see
Who shows me his white teeth & brown skin joy

Go find my old friend we'll go to the museum
Talk about politics with the cats and ask for revolution
Get back on the plane & chant high in the sky
Back to Earth to New York Garbage streets fly

Im gonna come back with Frightens in the heart
At New York's electric eternity here
Pull the airconditioner plug from the wall
Sit down with my straight spine and Pray!

I'm going down to Puerto Rico
I'm going down on the midnight plane
I'm going down on the Vomit Express
I'm going down with my suitcase pain.

Nov. 17, '71

GOING TO SAN DIEGO

Come to San Diego, whole world gonna swing
I'm going to San Diego Let them brass bells ring
O Mister San Diego, find out what my Future bring

Gona San Diego, walk out on that street
Gona San Diego, hello who Ever I meet
Goin there happy Gonna take my lonely feet

Gonna San Diego Salute your holy soul
Salute San Diego Shake your jelly roll
Republican Convention there be a great big fruit bowl

Gonna San Diego—Announce the end of the War
Gonna San Diego—ain't gonna murder no more
Tell them politicians stop acting like a whore

Gonna San Diego—raise a holy cry
Gonna San Diego—Sing like I could die
O Lord let there be Tears in every Eye

Gonne to San Diego Gonne to San Diego
Gonne to San Diego Gonne to San Diego
Gonne to San Diego Gonne to San Diego
Gonne to San Diego Gonne to San Diego

Gonne to San Diego gonna take my blues along
Gonna San Diego—sing a peaceful Song
Oh San Diego, I won't do no wrong

Come to San Diego Show you're a peaceful man
Old Mr. Nixon better bow down to Uncle Sam
All them Citizens best elect the Lamb

Nov. 17, 1971

3

JIMMY BERMAN RAG

Whozat Jimmie Berman
I heard you drop his name?
Whadd'ze got to say
what papers is he sellin?
I dont know if he's the guy
I met or aint the same—
Well that Jimmie Berman was
a boy that is worth tellin':

Jimmie Berman on the corner
Sold the New York Times
Jimmie Berman in New York
He had a long long Climb—

Started as a shoeshine boy
Ended on Times Square—
Jimmie Berman whatzat rose
You got settin' in your hair?

Jimmie Berman what's your sex
Why ya hang round here all day?
Jimmie Berman What Love Next
O What (God) do you pray?

Who you wanna sleep with tonite Jimmie Boy
Would'ya like—Come with me?
Jimmy Berman—O my love,
Oh what misery—

Jimmie Berman do you feel
the same as what I do
Jimmy Berman wont you come home
And make love with me too?

Jimmie Berman I'll take my clothes off
Lay me down in bed
Jimmy Berman drop your pants
I'll give you some good head

Eighteen year old Jimmie!
The Boy is my delight!
Eighteen year old Jimmy
I'll love him day and night!

Now I know I'm getting kinda old
To chase poor Jimmy's tail
But I wont tell your other loves—
It be too long a tale.

Jimmy Berman please love me
I'll throw myself at your feet—
Jimmy Berman I'll give you money O
Wont that be neat!

Jimmie Berman just give me
your heart and yeah your soul
Jimmy Berman please come home
With me I would be whole

Jimmie Berman on the street
Waitin for his god!
Jimmy Berman as I pass
Gives me a holy nod.

Jimmy Berman he has watched
And seen the Strangers pass—
Jimmy Berman he gave up—
He wants no more of ass.

Jimmy Berman does yoga

He smokes a little grass,
Jimmie Berman's back is straight,
He knows what to bypass—

Jimmy Berman dont take Junk
He dont shoot speed neither
Jimmie Berman's got a healthy mind
And Jimmy Berman is Ours—

Jimmy Berman, Jimmy Berman
I will say Goodbye
Jimmy Berman Jimmy Berman
Love you till I die—

Jimmy Berman Jimmy Berman
Wave to me as well—
Jimmy Berman Jimmy Berman
We've abolished Hell!

Nov. 17, 1971

MANY LOVES

Old rumors...

Many people I know are dead
Many people with whom I was in bed
Many souls I know underground
Many heroes I'll—never found

My first love Neal Cassidy
He ran away from me
Second love Kerouac
He began to drink, alack

Peter the third
        took Speed quite long
    (quite long quite long quite long)
He's back in the World now
        doing no wrong
    (food growing food growing food)

Many loves are underground
Many loves make no more sound
Many loves are gone to the sky
Many loves have said goodbye

Nov. 20, 1971

4 AM BLUES

Oh when you gonna
             lie down by my side
When the spirit hits you
             please lie down by my side
Three nights you didnt come home
             I slept by myself & sighed

O when you gonna
             look me in the eyes
When the spirit hits you
             look me in the eyes
Oh honey come hug me
             take me by surprise

Take me by surprise
             come home, lie down by my side
Away three days
             Sometimes I cried
Lie here alone
             Heart open wide

Gone another night
             Hand on my heart close my eye
You dont want me in your arms
             dont want to hear me sigh
That's how I'm alone,
             That's how I'm going to die.

Dec. 20, 71
(Traum Folk Concert)

New York Blues

NEW YORK BLUES

Walking blues (andante)

I live in an apartment, sink leaks thru the walls
Lower Eastside full of bedbugs, Junkies in the halls
House been broken into, Tibetan Tankas stole
Speed freaks took my statues, made my love a fool
    Speed freaks took my statues, made my love a fool

Days I came home tired   nights I needed sleep
Cockroaches crawled in bed with me   my brain began to creep
My work was never done,   my rest'll never begin
I'll be dead and buried and never pleasure win
    I'll be dead and buried and never pleasure win

Lover boy threw meat at me   cursed the day we met
Speed freaks and bedbugs   New York City's what you get
Someday they'll build subways   get rid of all the cars
Cops kill all the bedbugs   speed freaks land on Mars
    Cops kill all the bedbugs   speed freaks land on Mars

December 1971

11

NY Youth Call Annunciation

NY YOUTH CALL ANNUNCIATION

Come all you Jewish boy friends
       that live here in New York
For years we have been reading
       your delicatessen talk
Now it's time to enter
       our bodies and to scream
Now's the time to wake up from
       the International Dream

Two generations ye've hidden
       your light & your sex
Your parents starved to master matter & your
       consciousness perplex
Now all these matter-junkies
       are lost in Moloch's maw
You're left alone in Universe
       your habits to withdraw

Come all ye black boys
       that live on New York's streets
Slaved for decades in Harlem
       Beat & jailed by police
Rise up ye rainbow consciousness
       over Manhattan Isle
Let Loose the joy of mastery ye've
       conquored the white style —

Come all ye Puerto Rican cats
       exiled from tropic sun
To labor in the ice and soot of
       poisonous Capitalism
Beat your drums & chang guitars
       Proclaim your softest joy
You will not drink from white beer cans
       nor be his junkey Boy

Come all ye AmerIndians
                    that drink in Brooklyn's bars
Let loose your ancient Buffalo cry
                    chant under Sand Street's stars
Redeem the Mental Nation
                    Wake the Great Mother's corpse
Human bodies ye are still
                    Whatever Iron warps —

Come O poet Italians
                    long scared of the Syndicate
Secret death and blackmail
                    made your brains work late
Sing over rooftops your
                    ancient Cumaean blues
Dance with your Afric Brothers
                    the world's old tender news

Come out yer Greeks & Russians
                    Ye Arabs & ye Slavs
Boogie woogie down Broadway
                    weep tears of many loves
America was lost
                    ye children found her again
Squatting on the planet
                    belly full of metal sin

Highways full of speed
                    Brain city full of junk
Television blew her mind
                    her eyes are plastic gunk
Every little scream she made
                    was cause for planet war
O soulful Eastern boys & girls
                    lead home our Mother Whore

O Polish boys jumped up

from Cleveland Chicago Seed

Stop eating meat   Kielbasa

sausage lonely greed

One acres grainy labor,

or one acre of Green

Yields insteada pigs

twenty times the same protein

White boys of Manhattan

White girls of New York

Come gather all together

your Loves for the Great Work

Kneel down adore your brothers

& sisters of the soul & skin

Lay hands on all your bodies

your touch makes the world kin

O come ye children that grew up

New York around your ears

This century ends with Brimstone

or else your tender tears

Gather vigor in heart

gather intellect into your brains

When God stiffens your spine

Only emotion remains

Dec. 20, 1971

Come Back Xmas

radiator cockroach waving your horns at the wall, what'll I feed you I

don't eat meat at all. go tell the bed bug he better stay out in

the hall

COME BACK CHRISTMAS

CHRISTMAS COME BACK
        NEW YORK CITY DIED LAST YEAR
NEW YEAR COME BACK
        BIG CITY DIED LAST YEAR
DEAD ON HER BIG STONE FEET
        NO LIGHTBULB SHED ONE TEAR

O MISTER SANTA CLAUS
        HOW COME YA STILL COMING ROUND
HISTORIC REINDEER
        FLYING THE SAME OLD GROUND
ANYWAY YOU NORTHPOLE PEOPLES
        SURE MAKE A PRETTY SOUND —

BRING ME A BIG MASS TRANSPORT
        GARBAGE DISPOSAL SYSTEM TOO
CLEAN MY POLICE FORCE
        SO MY BOY FRIENDS WONT SNIFF SO MUCH GLUE
& I'LL START GIVING PRESENTS
        & THANK YOU FOR COMING IN BLUE

LAST YEAR I THOUGHT
        I'LL NEVER LEAVE MANHATTAN ALIVE
YEAR BEFORE BROUGHT UP
        MY VOMIT ON RIVERSIDE DRIVE
NEXT YEAR IF I'M HERE
        I THINK I'LL BRING MY BEE HIVE

HONEY OH HONEY
        I KNOW I'M MAKING NO SENSE
SWEET MOLASSES FORGIVE
        MY ANTI WAR GRUNTS
SUGAR BABY THIS CITY
        STOLE MY POETRY PANTS

MERRY CHRISTMAS
           DONT TAKE TOO MUCH HARD DOPE
HAPPY NEW YEAR
           DONT HANG YOURSELF WITH A ROPE
MANAHATTA REBORN
           AFTER WE GAVE UP ALL HOPE

RADIATOR COCKROACH
           WAVING YOUR HORNS AT THE WALL
WHAT'LL I FEED YOU
           I DONT EAT MEAT AT ALL
GO TELL THE BEDBUG
           HE BETTER STAY OUT IN THE HALL

                    December 1971
                    (At St. Mark's Church)

18

MACDOUGAL STREET BLUES

Sitting inna basement
        Macdougal Street guitar factory
Sitting in Feenjon's Greenwich Village
        Banjo University
Every boy here's a genius
        plays the guitar except me

Fourty five years I wanted to be
        minstrel man
Dictated epics in books inside a
        Volkswagon van
Grey hair on my head   I'm
        singing the best that I can

O Mr Garbageman dont take me away
        No   not yet
O Mr Garbageman dont   dump truck me
        like an old cigarette
Not till I   pick out a
        Song you'll never forget

I tried singing Mantras   I
        tried singing out William Blake
Tried Mantra chanting   Ah
        tried tuning up old holy Blake
Now I'll sing Him the blues if   Good
        God gives me a break

Back in the basement, Guitars
        ringing all around
Screaming in a basement
        Guitars ring me all around
I can only play three chords   I can
        still sing my way underground

Listen here Children   I'm an
        old creep full of desire
I got a big mouth   It's
        because my heart is on fire
If I can get hot   you could
        sing like an Angel Choir.

                    January 1972

CIA DOPE CALYPSO

IN NINETEEN HUNDRED   FOURTY-FIVE
CHINA WAS WON BY MAO TSE TUNG
CHIANG KAI SHEK'S ARMY   RAN AWAY
AND THEY'RE WAITING THERE   IN THAILAND TODAY

SUPPORTED BY THE   CIA
PUSHING JUNK   DOWN THAILAND WAY

FIRST THEY STOLE FROM THE   MEO TRIBES
UP IN THE HILLS THEY   STARTED TAKING BRIBES
THEN THEY SENT THEIR SOLDIERS   UP TO SHAN
COLLECTING OPIUM TO   SELL TO THE MAN

PUSHING JUNK IN BANGKOK TODAY
SUP/PORTED BY THE   C I A

BROUGHT THEIR JAM ON   MULE TRAINS DOWN
TO CHIANG RAI THAT'S   A RAILROAD TOWN
SOLD IT NEXT TO   POLICE CHIEF BRAIN
HE TOOK IT TO TOWN ON THE   CHOOCHOO TRAIN

TRAFFICKING DOPE TO   BANGKOK ALL DAY
SUP/PORTED BY THE   C I A

THE POLICEMAN'S NAME WAS   MR PHAO
HE PEDDLED DOPE GRAND SCALE AND HOW
CHIEF OF BORDER   CUSTOMS PAID
BY CENTRAL INTELLIGENCE'S   U.S. AID

THE WHOLE OPERATION,   NEWSPAPERS SAY
SUPPORTED BY THE   C.I.A.

HE GOT SO SLOPPY &   PEDDLED SO LOOSE
HE BUSTED HIMSELF &   COOKED HIS OWN GOOSE
TOOK THE REWARD FOR AN   OPIUM LOAD
SEIZING HIS OWN HAUL WHICH   SAME HE RESOLD

BIG TIME PUSHER A DECADE   TURNED GREY
WORKING FOR THE   CIA

THE WHOLE OPERATION   FELL INTO CHAOS
TILL U.S. INTELLIGENCE   CAME INTO LAOS
I'LL TELL YOU NO LIE   I'M A TRUE AMERICAN
OUR BIG PUSHER THERE WAS   PHOUMI NOSOVAN

ALL THEM PRINCES IN A   POWER PLAY
BUT PHOUMI WAS THE MAN FOR   THE CIA

TOUBY LYFONG HE   WORKED FOR THE FRENCH
BIG FAT MAN LIKE TO   DINE & WENCH
PRINCE OF THE MEOS   GREW BLACK MUD
OPIUM FLOWED THROUGH THE   LAND LIKE A FLOOD

COMMUNISTS CAME AND CHASED THE   FRENCH AWAY
SO TOUBY TOOK A JOB WITH   THE CIA

AND HIS BEST FRIEND   GENERAL VANG PAO
RAN OUR MEO ARMY LIKE   A SACRED COW
HELICOPTER SMUGGLERS FILLED   LONG CHENG'S BARS
IN XIENG QUANG PROVINCE ON   THE PLAIN OF JARS

IT STARTED IN SECRET   THEY WERE FIGHTING YESTERDAY
CLANDESTINE SECRET ARMY   OF THE CIA

ALL THROUGH THE 'SIXTIES   THE DOPE FLEW FREE
THRU TAN SON NHUT SAIGON   TO MARSHALL KY
AIR AMERICA   FOLLOWED THROUGH
TRANSPORTING CONFITURE   FOR PRESIDENT THIEU

ALL THESE DEALERS WERE   DECADES AND TODAY
THE INDOCHINESE MOB   OF THE U.S. CIA

OPERATION HAYLIFT OFFISIR WM COLBY
SAW MARSHALL KY FLY OPIUM   MR MUSTARD TOLD ME
INDOCHINA DESK   HE WAS CHIEF OF DIRTY TRICKS
"HITCH-HIKING" WITH DOPE PUSHERS
                                        WAS HOW HE GOT HIS FIX

SUBSIDIZING THE TRAFFICKERS   TO DRIVE THE REDS AWAY
NOW COLBY IS THE HEAD OF THE   WHOLE WORLD C.I.A.

                    January 1972

CIA Dope Calypso

ades   and   today   the   Indochinese   Mob   of   the   US   C I A .

TROOST STREET BLUES

You can teach me baby,
                    you can touch my soul
You can have my mouth,
                    you can have my jellyroll
Gimmie your heart baby
                    fuck me up my asshole

You can kiss my lips in Kansas
                    Belly naked on mine
You can suck my tongue
                    or suck my cock so fine
I love to put my tongue up in
                    your sweet behind

There's frightened deafed white folks
                    in Kansas City
Walter's Crescendo Lounge here
                    is my place to be
I have a bed on Troost Street,
                    back in Eternity

I can't find my words,
                    my feelings are unreal
I used to sit by your bedside
                    your prick I love to steal
Your belly's in an ash urn
                    Now how do I feel?*

Kansas City, got the blues
                    Early midnight Walter's bar
Years later sitting by the jukebox
                    how funky people are
But O them black musicians make me
                    feel like a soul star

I'm back in Kansas City
                    with my old time used-to-be
Alone with my Alone
                    that's the story you and me
I once met Lester Young
                    and got down on my knees

Bodies rot and faces vanish
                    Lips turn white
I had my dreams my love is dead
                    O Heaven it's all right
Here I am in Kansas City
                    I think I'll spend an empty night

*See "On Neal's Ashes," p. 99, *Fall of America,* City Lights, S.F. 1973

Put Down Yr Cigarette Rag

Don't   smoke   don't   smoke   don't smoke   don't   smoke   don't

smoke   don't   smoke   don't   smoke   don't   smoke   it sa

nine   billion   dollar   cap'tilost joke   don't   smoke   don't   smoke   don't

smoke   don't   smoke   don't   smoke   don't   smoke   don't   smoke   don't   smoke

Smoking makes you cough, you   can't   sing   straight, you   gargle   on   saliva   and   you

vomit   on   your   plate   don't   smoke   don't   smoke   don't .....

PUT DOWN YR CIGARETTE RAG

Dont smoke dont smoke dont smoke
Dont smoke
It's a nine billion dollar
Capitalist joke
            Dont smoke dont smoke dont smoke dont smoke

Smoking makes you cough,
you cant sing straight
You gargle on saliva
& vomit on your plate
            Dont smoke Dont smoke dont smoke dont smoke

You smoke in bed
You smoke on the hill
Smoke till yr dead
You smoke in Hell
            Dont smoke dont smoke Dope Dope
                        Dont smoke

You puff your fag
You suck your butt
You choke & gag
Teeth full of crud
            Smoke smoke smoke smoke Dont Dont Dont
                        Dont Dope Dope Dont Smoke

You pay your half buck
    for a deathly pack
Trust your bad luck
    & smoke in the sack—
            Dont Smoke Dont Smoke Nicotine Nicotine No
                        Smoke Dope Dope

275 Million in Green
'swat Madison Avenue gets
't advertise nicotine
& hook you radical brats
            Dont Smoke Dont Smoke Dont Smoke Nope Nope Dope Dope
                      Hoax Hoax Hoax Hoax

Black magic pushes dope
Sexy chicks in cars
America loses hope
& smokes and drinks in bars
            Dont smoke dont smoke dont smoke dont smoke dont dont dont dont
                      choke choke choke choke

Nine billion bucks a year
a Southern Industry
Buys Senator Joe Fear
who runs the CIA
          Dope smokes dope smokes dont smoke dont smoke cloak cloak cloak &
                    dagger cloak cloak cloak
               smoke smoke smoke smoke

Nine billion bucks for dope
approved by Time & Life
America's lost hope
The President smokes his wife
          Dont Smoke dont smoke dont smoke dont smoke dont smoke nope
                    nope nope nope

If you will get in bed
& give your girlfriend head
then you wont want a fag
Nor evermore a drag
          dont Smoke dont smoke Hope Hope Hope Hope Dont smoke O Please
                    Dont Smoke Dont Smoke
                    O Please O Please O Please
                    I'm calling on my knees

Twenty four hours in bed
& give your boyfriend head
Put Something in your mouth
Like skin not cigarette filth
          Suck tit suck tit suck tit suck cock suck cock suck clit suck prick
                    but dont smoke dont smoke dont smoke
                         nicotine it's too obscene dont Smoke nicotine
                         suck cock suck prick suck tit suck clit suck it
                              But don't smoke shit nope nope nope nope
                                   Dope Dope Dope Dope

Make believe yer sick
Stay in bed and lick
yr cigarette habit greed
one day's all you need
          In deed in deed in deed in deed smoke weed smoke weed but dont
                    smoke smoke smoke
                         dont smoke dont smoke
                              hope hope hope hope Nicotine dont
                                   smoke hope dont dont dont
                                        Dope Dope Dope Dope

                    (Improvise further)

                         March 1972

Slack Key Guitar

Sweet O-a-hu got pet-ro-le-um super high ways glass ho-tels, old Hi-wa-ii's buried un der Steamboat Mu-seum's Sugar Hells-- Bishop Estates leases homesites to the Kai-ser in-dus-try and the Mili-tary High-way's closed off to the ocean over Kole Ko-le.

SLACK KEY GUITAR

Sweet Oahu
   Got petroleum
      Superhighways
         Glass hotels,

Old Hawaii's
   buried under
      Steamboat Museum's
      Sugar Hells—

Bishop Estates
   Leases homesites
      to the Kaiser
      Industry

& the Military
   Highway's closed off
      to the ocean
         over Kole Kole.

March 1, 1972

FLYING TO FIJI

High up in the Space Ship orange sky glow
Streaks thru the cloud fringes, flying we go
To Fiji in the Pacific where hundreds of years
White men slaved black men, mixed money & tears

Blue lights the sky, cloud fringes stand still
Crags on horizon float silent, God's will
is empty for thousands of miles around
Blue clouds drift toward Sunrise ocean's blue ground

Now the great dome lights clear the blue day
Misted cloudshadows haze ocean floor grey
Ah the grey clouds like Leviathan flow
Along great horizons and hide sun eye glow

Metal wing trembles O hear Engines roar
At last the Gold sun boils on cloud shore
Brighter & Brighter gold glows in blue sky
Cloud tips & cloud drifts shine oh! the gold eye!

What Island's below us, not seen there before,
Great coral reef blasted up from last War?
Soon we will land on grey paradise isles
Ghost sailors come with dollars & smiles

Oh ho all ye hearties that fly thru the air
Look on the bright planet, see Fiji down there!
Green fields are furrowed, calm rivers flow
Farmlands & green mountains, the plane circles low.

March 2, 1972 6 am

POSTCARD TO D————

Chuggling along in an old open bus
     past the green sugarfields
         down a dusty dirt road
             overlooking the ocean in Fiji,
thinking of your big Macdougal street house
     & the old orange peels
         in your mail-garbage load,
             smoggy windows you clean with a squeejee——

March 3, 1972

34

REEF MANTRA

...Blue Starfish
       Violet minnow,
              Sea cucumber
                    Coral tide...

               March 3, 1972

SIRATOKA BEACH CROON

I

I closed my eyes on Fiji's sands
& what did I think of next?
You O big ear'd listener
& the Prajnaparamita text.

I thought of Herman Melville's rhyme
on olden Marquesa's shore
& dead Jack Kerouac's choochoo time
in modern Microphone roar.

A light rose up my body & spine
as children ripples fell —
Smiling head, that Consciousness
reached all my teachers in Hell.

O Music that washes from shore to shore
O Rhythm turned centuries old
Sing thru our mouths & wake the great Mind
The Bard's first chanting foretold.

II

I opened my eyes on Fiji's sands
What does the sunlight reveal?
Coral bones on the tiny grass beach
Flies on my hand wash and kneel —

Crabs in brown valleys of sand
Tree elbows leaned on the sea
Australian children yelling at wavelets
A rowboat in shade of the tree

Peaceful chatter of baby waves
Whitecaps' distant reef roar
Birds whistling thru green palm arms
Jeep tires speeding the shore.

O presence as timid as a white dog
That swims on the shallow tide
Salute O blue ocean in Heaven
Thru which our war bombers ride.

                    March 3, 1972
                    Fiji

BUS RIDE BALLAD ROAD TO SUVA

O ho for the bus that rolls down the dirt road
O ho the green sunlight that holds the dust cloud
O ho for the thin-mustached boy with his wound
O ho for banana trees crowding the ground!

O ho the Australian lad drest in red
O ho the Ferlinghetti, beard on his head,
O ho for the roar of the motor uphill
O ho for the feathery grass standing still!

O ho the palm islands that rise from blue sea
O ho the breezy sky that hangs over me
O ho the dirt road that gives us a way
To Fiji, Port Suva, we go there today!

O ho the black ladies so big and so fat
From eating the Taro-root, pink hair, no hat,
O ho the clean Indian wives in white cloth
O ho the green frog that ate the black moth!

O ho misty hills all Sun-shining we've seen
O ho palm-roof huts with doorsteps grass green
O ho the black cow head bent on the field —
Here by the old banyan, bus stops squeaky-wheeled!

The Fiji boy opens the beer with his teeth
The bottle sits down on the floor by his feet,
A cowrie-shell purse & Pall Mall cigarette —
Low tide by the ocean road, sand is still wet!

Green craggy M'Benga sits on the low sea
Her men walk thru fire for you & for me,
O ho that last night the round Kava bowl
Numbed my mouth tasting the island's strange soul!

O ho for hibiscus, mail pouch on the nail,
O ho for the palm frond that waves at the whale,
O ho tin roof deserts & drain pipes in rows —
Pacific Development Corp. only knows!

O ho blessed freedom on Fiji's green land
O ho virgin hills coconuts in your hand,
O ho bless the pawpaw & orchid that grows —
O ho bless the Englishman's leftover Rose!

But curst be the Murchesson Company cranks
Capitalists hiding behind Hong Kong's banks,
Curst be Pan Am & the Hotel Airways,
Their business is ruin for Edens always.

The wind that flaps the banana leaf Ho!
Cocks that peck in the garden & crow,
O ho for the switchbacks on red dirt hill sides
Cows walk by the jungle & grazing abide!

We roll over mountains, rocks clank in the dust,
Stop for bananas and pee as we must,
O ho the blue ocean! What green peak we passed?
Down there the white houses of Suva at last!

March 4, 1972
(1—4—1—5—1 Chord Changes)

Bus Ride Ballad Road to Suva

(last verse)

G

we) roll over mountains, rocks clank in the dust, stop for bananas and

pee as we must. Here's the blue ocean! what green peak we passed? Down

there the white houses of Suva at last!

Tear Gas Rag

Tear gas tear gas Tear gas tore my throat can't say my mantra

Tear gas got my goat Tear gas O lord tear gas I can't find my mind

Bombing North Viet-nam I'm stumbling around blind, Tear gas in Boulder

Tear gas in my heart frightened on college hill by Nixon's poison fart

Tear gas here tear gas there Colo-rado and Saigon. They'll be droppin' tear gas every

time I get a hard on

TEAR GAS RAG
Old Southern Rag, Blind Blake

Tear Gas Tear Gas
Tear gas tore my throat
Can't say my mantra
Tear Gas got my goat

Tear Gas O Lord Tear Gas
I can't find my mind
Bombing North Vietnam
I'm stumbling around blind

Tear Gas in Boulder
Tear Gas in my heart
Frightened on college hill
Nixon's poison Fart

Tear Gas here Tear Gas there
Colorado and Saigon
They'll be droppin teargas
Everytime I get a hardon.

May 10, 1972
Ft. Collins, Colorado

43

BLUE GOSSIP

I guess he got sick of having to get up and get
            scared of being shot down
Also probably he got sick of
            being a methedrine clown;
Also he wanted to go back explore
            Macdougal Street New York town

I guess he got sick of a Cosmic
            consciousness too abstract
I guess he wanted to go back
            t'his own babies' baby shit fact
Change his own children's diapers not get lost
            in a transcendental Rock & Roll act.

I guess he thought maybe he had
            enough gold for the world
Saw red white & blue big enough now
            needn't be further unfurled
I guess he felt prophet show good example,
            bring himself down in the world.

I guess he took Zen Chinese vows
            and became an anonymous lout
I guess he figured he better step down off stage
            before he got kicked out
I guess he felt lonesome and blue
            and he wanted out.

I guess he did what anyone
            sens'ble would do
Otherwise like Mick Jagger go out on stage
            wearing curtains of blue
And fly around the world with great big
            diamonds and pearls made of glue.

I guess he felt he'd used up
                    'nuff of the 'lectric supply
I guess he knew that the Angel
                    of Death was nigh—
I guess he sighed his
                    next mortal sigh.

I guess he guessed he could
                    find out his own mortal face
I guess he desired to examine
                    his own family place
I guess he decided to act with
                    more modest *silent* grace

I guess he decided to learn
                    from ancient tongue
So he studied Hebrew
                    as before he blabbed from his lung
I guess he required to learn new
                    tender kind songs to be sung.

I guess he thought he was not guru
                    for Everyone's eyes
He must have seen Vajra Hells
                    in old visions he'd devised
He must've seen infernal assassins
                    stealing his garbage supplies.

I guess he decided to die
                    while still alive
In that way, ancient death-in-life,
                    saints always thrive
Above all remember his children
                    he already pickd a good wife.

I guess he decided to Be
                    as well as sing the blues

I guess he decided like Prospero
                    to throw his white magic wand into the Ocean blue—
Burn up all his magic books,
                    go back to Manhattan, think something new.

I guess he decided like Prospero
                    World was a dream
Every third thought is grave
                    or so Samsara would seem—
Took Hebrew Boddhisatva's vow
                    and saw golden light death agleam.

I guess he decided he
                    did not need to be More Big
I guess he decided he was not the
                    Great Cosmic Thingamajig
I guess he decided to end that sweet song
                    and such is his Suchness I dig.

                    Oct. 23, 1972 Davidson College

THE HOUSE OF THE RISING SUN

There's been a house in New Orleans
                 they call the Rising Sun
And it's been the ruin of many a poor boy
                 and God I know I'm one

I sailed down there in '45
                 tryin to get my body laid
I could not get my pecker up
                 and Lord I felt betrayed

It was my first time on a ship
                 w/ Puerto Rican men
I'll smoke their marijuana but
                 never go to their whorehouse again

That girl was pretty young & cold
                 I lay down on her in bed
She waited naked for my act
                 lay there like a corpse new dead

And since that day I sucked the cocks
                 of a couple hundred boys
The Rising Sun has set on me
                 the man in the moon's my joys

Yeh since that day I sucked the cocks
                 of a hundred teenage souls
Lord I'll trade the House of the Rising Sun
                 for a Peghouse w/ a Hundred Holes.

Dec. 23, 1972

Everybody Sing

EVERYBODY SING

Everybody's just   a little
      bit homo sexual
         whether they like it or not
Everybody feels   a little bit
      of love for the boys
         even if   they almost forgot

Everybody goes   a little
      bit sweet hearted
         for a poor freckled sun faced lad
Y'all give him   a little
      bit of your soul
         like a girl that's never been had

Now everybody everybody
      everybody knows
         how thrilling a kiss can be
right on the mouth
      no thought no doubt
         from that singing boy from Tennessee—

Everybody knows   what it
      is to fall in love
         with the football hero bold
But so everybody's thought
      never do get lost
         God remembers when you're growing old.

Everybody's born   just a
      little bit gay
         a little bit fairy, and a dog
Everybody's born a lordly
      King of May and a
         little bit even of a hawg.

So if you can't get with your
            natural human
                        and dont want no part queer
You line yourself up against
            the wall with your ghosts
                        and shoot to kill your fear.

You can empty your revolver
            in any woman's cunt
                        or any man's mouth you despise
You can call whore names
            or play fairy games
                        like gouging out Vietnamese eyes,

But you'll never get laid
            by a lady or a maid
                        who won't be scared of your thighs
No you'll never get laid
            but with money you paid
                        to buy off your woman with lies,

No you'll never get laid
            and see freely displayed
                        the Goddess that comes in disguise—

So if you're in trouble
            and dont like your double
                        why dontcha come see me?
I'll take you by the hand
            and love you through the land
                        and ease your tender misery.

Feb. 4, 1973

50

PRAYER BLUES

When you break your leg
        there's nothing to stand on
Break your leg
        There's nothing to stand on
Break yr bones,
        nothing to stand on
Break up your body
        Nowhere to be.

Jesus Christ
        Nowhere to be
Jesus Christ
        Show me
Jesus Christ
        show me the way to go home
Jesus Christ
        Show mercy to me.

Jesus Christ
        Didn't they break yr bones
Jesus Christ
        Didn't you weep & you groan
Up on the cross
        Didn't you feel alone?
O crown of thorns,
        Hear sweet Jesus' moans.

Jesus is His name   (Jesus Christ)
        As good   as any   (Jesus Christ)
Yes Jackie dear   Jesus' name
        is good   as any   (Jesus Christ)
When your body's in pain   (Shift the load to the Lord)
        and your heart is empty   (Shift the load to the Lord)
O sacred Heart   (Jesus Christ)
        One God is plenty   (Shift the load to the Lord)

Lord Jesus Come   (Jesus Christ)
          Come in my heart   (Shift the load to the Lord)
Lord Jesus Come   (Jesus Christ)
          Come in my heart   (Shift the load to the Lord)
Lord Jesus Come   (Jesus Christ)
          Come in my heart   (Load to the Lord)
Lord Jeeesus
          Come in my heart

Milarepa Come   (Shift the load to the Lord)
          Come in my heart   (Shift the load to the Lord)
          . . . . etc.

Translator Marpa come   (Load to the Lord)
          Come in my heart   (Shift the load to the Lord)
Naropa Come   (Shift the Load to the Lord)
          Come in my heart   (Shift the Load to the Lord)
Tilopa Come   (Shift the load to the Lord)
          Come in my heart   (Shift the Load to the Lord)
Vajradhara   (Dorje Chang)
          Come in my heart   (Om Ah Hūm)

There aint noone left   I can
          Come to in my bones
There aint nobody left
          I can come to in my bones
There aint noone here   I can
          come to in my bones
Aint no One anywhere   I can
          come to with my bone

Get rid of it all fast   (Jesus Christ)
          Credit cards in the sun   (Load O Lord)
Unload   Unload!
          house & books   everyone   (Load to the Lord)
Sell it all! Give it all away   your
          farm's no longer funny   (Jesus Christ)
Dump your ego
          & ruin Wall Street's money!   (Shift the load to the Lord)

52

Shift the load to God   (Shift the load to the Lord)
        Let Him worry 'bout the Books   (Load to the Lord)
Give it up ! Let be!   Lord you'll love
        the President's looks (Shift the load to the Lord)
Throw it all away   Begone! to
        Saigon's Generals & crooks   (Load to the Lord)
Dont be so smart!   Get lost!   Last Supper,
        too many cooks! (Shift the load to the Lord)

Shift the load to the Lord   (Shift the load to the Lord)
        Let Him worry about the War   (Load to the Lord)
Shift the Load to the Lord!   (Shift the load to the Lord)
        I cant fight any more!   (Lord to the Lord)
Shift the load to the Lord!   (Shift the Load to the Lord)
        The Soul is a Whore!   (Load to the Lord!)
Shift the load to the Lord!   (Shift the load to the Lord!)
        My soul is no more! (Om Ah Hūm)

Jesus Christ   (Shift the Load to the Lord)
        Take away my pain   (Shift the Load to the Lord)
Jesus Christ   (Shift the load to the Lord)
        Forgive me again   (Shift the load to the Lord)
Please Master   (Load to the Lord)
        You can have my Fame   (Load to the Lord)
JOD HE VOV HE
        I submit to your Name.

                    February 1973

Prayer Blues

Broken Bone Blues

Broken Bone Bone Bone   All over the ground Broken

Bone Bone Bone   Every where the sound of Broken Bone Bone Bone

Every one brought down   Ev-'ry one brought down   To Broken

Bone Bone Bone Broken   Head and boney crown

BROKEN BONE BLUES

"Naropa, your clay pitcher of a body,
believing in an I, deserves to be
broken..."

—Marpa, *Naropa* (Guenther
transl. Oxford '63)

Broken   Bone   Bone   Bone
    All over the Ground
Broken   Bone   Bone   Bone
    Everywhere the Sound
of Broken Bone Bone Bone
    Everyone brought down
    Everyone brought down

to broken   Bone Bone Bone
    Broken head & bony crown
Broken Bone Bone Bone
    Broken guru-king & clown
Broken Bone Bone Bone
    To the Boneyard I am bound
    To the Boneyard I am bound

Broken heart   Broken toe
    Broken Soul   Broken nose
Broken heaven   Broken woe
    Broken body into broken
Earth must go
    into broken
        earth must go.

When my bones all break
    I must feel my way to Death
When all my bones break
    when my meat starts to scrape

57

Through Death I will escape
      to Heaven through my heart
      to Heaven thru my heart's breath

Broke my leg under my knee
      Broke my heart   broke my greed
Broke my body like a dog
      Like a scared dog indeed
Broke my dumb body
      so God could see me
      So God could see me he broke my body.

Broken Bones O Lord
      I'll give my house away
Broken bones O God
      It was never mine anyway
Broken Bones O Buddha
      Take my skull today
      Or Take back my skull someday

Break   Break   Break
      O bones every where
Break   Break   Break
      O Soul in the black air
Break   Break   Break
      My body, God take care.
      My body, God take good care.

Take your time O Lord
      Break my bones ten times ten
Take your time O Death
      And you can tell me when
Farewell swift body dream
      God bless me again,
      Come down God, bless me again
      & I'll come back & bless you again.

February 1973

"WHEN I WOKE UP THIS MORNING"

When I woke up this morning   Cambodia was bombed again
It made me mad   I felt so sad
and Nixon did not even   tell the reason why
O how do you like to hear bombs falling year after year?
I guess them bombs won't stop until they fall on our ear
because when I woke up this morning   Cambodia was bombed again

O when I woke up this morning   Cambodia was bombed again
From 1965   you see   to 1973
One million   nine hundred thousand   souls have died
A million seven hundred thousand bodies   wounded year after year
Thirteen million homeless from the bombs   did you hear?
A million homeless from the bombs   did you hear?
Cause when I woke up this morning   Cambodia was bombed again

Lord when I woke up this morning   Cambodia was bombed again
O what a merciless rain! Seven million tons of pain—
The President did not even   have a legal reason   why
Hundred thirty-five Billion dollars already it cost—
What Karma remains?   What Merit is lost?
Because when I woke up this morning   Cambodia was bombed again!

Yeah when Allah woke up this morning   Cambodia was bombed again,
Lord when Jesus woke up this morning   Cambodia was bombed again,
Lord when Mary woke up this morning   Cambodia was bombed again,
When Buddha woke up this morning   Cambodia was bombed again,
and when we woke up this morning   Cambodia was bombed again.

Music & Words by Jim Jackson,
adapted by Peter Orlovsky & A.G.
April 1973

ON READING DYLAN'S WRITINGS

Now that it's dust and ashes
now that it's human skin
Here's to you Bob Dylan
a poem for the laurels you win

Sincerest form of flattery
is imitation they say
I've broke my long line down
to write a song your way

Those "chains of flashing images"
that came to you at night
were highest farm boys' day dreams
that glimpse the Angels' light

And tho the dross of wisdom's come
and left you lone on earth
remember when the Angels call
your soul for a new birth

It wasnt dope that gave you truth
no money that you stole
—was God himself that entered in
shining your heavenly soul.

July, 27 1973
London

STAY AWAY FROM THE WHITE HOUSE

Stay away from the White House
> Stay away I wish you well
Stay away from the White House
> Stay away I wish you well
Stay away from the White House
> Or you'll go to Vajra Hell

Stay away from New York City
> It costs money to live there
Stay away from the country
> The banks own all the air
Stay away from their electric
> It'll whiten your beard hair

Stay away from smoking cigarettes
> Stay away stay away
Stay your hand off your Marlboro
> Stay away stay away
Stay away from nicotine & beer
> It'll make you old and gay

Stay away from fucking broomsticks
> It'll give you syphilis
Stay away from fucking rubber dolls
> even if they got big tits
Stay away from 14 year old boys
> fuckem once they call it quits

Stay away Stay away O yes yes stay away
from eating chemical donuts for breakfast yesterday
Stay away from living death tho the Army gives good pay

Stay away from Capitalism and the bosses' CIA
Stay away from Oil Industry they rob your energy
Stay away from Secret Policeman
               when he calls you out to play

Yea stay away from Satan in the good old USA
Stay away from eating meatballs
               while the Wall Street Dodgers play
Stay away from the White House this year,
               wish you a fine day.

Stay away Stay away away from all that jive
rippen off the niggers just to keep the band alive
Yes rippen off the nigger, how white musicians thrive

Stay away from all them jewboys with their Zionist delights
Stay away from all them Christians calling all them jewboys Kikes
Stay away from all them prophets, they'll get you into fights

Stay away from all them Arabs with that murder on their mind
Stay away from State Department they bow and scrape you blind
Stay away from Rockefeller he blows up an oily wind

Stay away from Richard Nixon he'll get you all in jail
He'll kick you and he'll punch you & he'll make your vision fail
and while he's got you staying away
               from the White House he will wail

"O Stay away from my White House I got it all my own
You can hear it in the basement
               all them singing Plumbers groan
Stay away O all you Democrats except the Hawks I've blown

You can come into my White House Senator Jackson Hawk
You're the one that loves the Army Billions you wont balk
Mr Ford and C.I.A. Colby right in my door you walk."

Stay away from Nirvana your ambition makes you blind
Stay away from Brahma Loka, you can only grasp the wind
Stay away from every Heaven you'll wake up in suffering Mind

Come down! Yeeeaah! Come down to earth right here
on Avenue C & Tenth street make your mind icy clear
Come down to Earth Merry Xmas I wish you a Happy New Year

Dec. 25, 1973

Stay Away from the White House

2 AM DIRTY JERSEY BLUES

I come from New Jersey and I love to suck your prick
I come from New Jersey you're the boy I surely pick
'F I were walking round Jersey City Looking for sumpen quick

I come from Paterson New Jersey & I like to make love fast
But the love I like to make is love that Forever'll last
That's why ever time I see you I bend down & kiss your ass.

I love them Jersey City boys Their bellies are so ruddy fine
Yeah them Jersey City boys have asses like sweet wine
Sucken Jersey City Cock's like sucken on a joint with my mind

Love your Jersey City Belly love your Jersey City breast
& in yr Jersey City arms O honey I take my sweetest rest
When I look into your Jersey City eyes all New Jersey is expressed

Do you love me a little Jersey City? Yeah you love me a lot!
O Jersey City boy I love you all I got
Gimme your Jersey City come I'll swallow on the spot

When I lie on your Jersey City heart taste your Jersey City kiss
I know sweet 21 year old boy New Jerseys of pure bliss
And if you dont believe me you dont know the fun you miss.

> Feb. 10, 1974
> (1—4—1—5—1 Chord Changes)

HARDON BLUES

Blues is like a hardon   comes right in your mouth
Blues is like a hardon,   it comes in your mouth
never know when its coming   in your North or in yr South

Yea Blues like a hardon, leads you down the road
Blues like a hardon, your standing on the road
Lord I gotta stop here, get rid of my weary load

Blues is like a hardon, it takes you far from home
Go out in night time, in streets & subways roam
looking for a lover like the blues who won't let you alone

Blues is like a hardon, I got a case of Blues
aint got clap or gonnorhea just got my hardon blues
If you were sitting here in bed with me you'd be the one I choose

Blues is like a hardon, I can't leave it alone
Sitting in my bed in Boulder, all I can do is groan
If I dont get it off right now, someday it'll all be gone.

Aug. 16, 1974

DOPE FIEND BLUES

Yes I'm a dope fiend, I dont believe your laws
Hey Mr Policeman I'm a dope fiend, take that
                                joint out of your jaws
I'm a dopefiend and I'm getting out of jail because

I'm a dopefiend sitting in my bedroom high
I didn't even light up no muggles, dont know why
I'm just naturally a dopefiend under empty sky

Yes I'm a dopefiend I dont sniff cocaine
I hear the walls ringing   my nose is still in pain
It's snowing all round NY City gimme a 2 penny plain

Oho I'm a dopefiend shoulda seen me usta mainline
Yah seen me shoulda shoot that white heroine
useta get the chills   but never burnt down my mind

Hey hey Oh Lord Dope Fiend I dropped LSD
I seen Manhattan's towers stick up in Eternity
Ten years ago you shoulda took the elevator up with me,
                                Holy!

Ha Ha I'm a dopefiend niggerlovin Commie Fagot Queen
I'm a beatnick hippie longhair but a square I never been
But if you Mother see my picture in the paper
                        she say I look clean

Hey I'm a dopefiend I'm a dopefiend I breathe sweet clean air
I dont shoot speed in my arm never more I'm a dopefiend everywhere
I'm a dopefiend in the policeman's eyes Yeah They wouldnt dare

to bust me for dopefiend I dont carry any shit around
I'm just a dopefiend by nature I like to sit on the ground
all naked with my clothes on   make a blue mantra sound

68

I'm a dopefiend I'm a dopefiend gonna bust this nation's mind
I'm gonna put LSD in your prayers & laughing gas in the wind
Aether & Peyote gonna drive Mt Ranier blind —

I'm a dopefiend I roll my soul in friendly grass
Dopefiend Dopefiend I carry Nothing   but Dharma up my ass
Yeaas all you dopefiends hear me!   out there in the middle class!

Hey rich dopefiend when you gonna change the laws?
Hey poor dopefiend join the Socialist Revolutionary party because
They gonna legalise existence, everybody ride a big white horse.

                    December 31, 1974

END VIETNAM WAR

Come along come along the end of Vietnam war
Dirty smart bombs and napalms & US Army whores
Come along come along hey baby don't be late
Come along come along, let's celebrate Watergate

Come along come along, poor Nixon's in his home
Come along come along, sitting under Teapot Dome
Come along come along, forget their heroin
Smoke some grass and relax & forget yr bloody wine

Come along o Americans & let's be Number two
Number one was a pissyassed act we all went through
Come along save the whales & save the humans too
and the ladies & the fairies & the communists true blue

Come along outa the cold war, the planet still is here
We got to save our momma, nothing worse we have to fear
Come along & let the people and other species rare
breathe again in vasty space the cleaned up U.S. air

Come along without your fission, & if you fusion choose
first make sure you don't burn up the very ground you use
Come along without your pistol, without your policeman's badge
Secret infiltrators shooting up themself in stupid rage

Come along without your police state
                    come along without your pow'r
Come along just as you are, really naked for an hour
You have all yr life to wear yr clothes,
                    80 years to milk your cow
Come along & breathe together & conspire
                    to be here now —

Come along come along the hour is at hand
When all this mighty Nation that Smokes across the land

Can wake up again & shake off our Indochina scream
and hear 800,000 orphan babies they all dream

Come along o mighty Nation & get down on your knees
and ask the Gods & angels to forgive us if they please
We have killed 2,000,000 people we have wounded millions more
And 15 million refugees are waiting out the door

So come along humble, and act to please mankind
Cut down on our electric whose dim light has
                              made us blind
to the stars and all the birdies & the Cayotes & the babes
We have seen without the seeing, buried under
                              brimstone waves

Come along come along, the war is over now
Indochina's independent & we are friends with Mao
The war is over YEEAH, the war is over here
and now begins the battle to make our souls
                              more dear

Come along come along, & empty out your mind
of all the American garbage we threw into the wind
All the Law & order chatter, that the gangsters sold us fools
All the military clatter, & their costly useless tools

We need more farms & farmers, we need to work the land
We need to get down on our knees and seed with our own hand
the earth we stand on top of, the earth we have bombed out
Come along come along, lift the sky with holy shout

Come along in Tallahassee, come along in Idaho
kick out the military cops   Let all secret agents go
To the unemployment office, down here with Us below.

                              April 21, 1975

GURU BLUES

I cant find anyone to show me what to do
I cant find anyone
                   It's maken me so blue
that I cant find anyone
                   anyone but you
O I cant find anyone that knows me
                     good as you
Yeah I cant find anyone,
                only you Guru

I cant find anyone that's visited the past
I cant find anyone
                 That's willing to be last
to take me up to heaven
               They're going to hell so fast
O I cant find anyone to blow me
               in the grass
Yeah I cant find anyone,
             fuck me in the ass

I cant find anyone
               That isn't drinking wine
I cant find a teacher
               That isnt loaded blind
I cant find anyone
               that isnt out of his mind
on ideas on Fears or the tears
               cops leave behind
Yeah I cant find anyone dont want to
             police the wind—

I cant find anyone that wants to meditate
Nobody wants to work, or play with a steady state
Economy, nobody wants
             the earth to celebrate

a world of conscious mercy, a world we could create
If we all sat down and decided not to be great.

I look in the White House, theres no one talks to me
I look in the Con gress
                    dont know Eternity
The Supreme Court
                    is fighting with the Sea
They're sitting now deciding on
                    the old death penalty
and the Rosenberg's children
                    have written their story

And what's the public doing
                    but drinking beer in cans
and what's the children screwing with
                    but cars to go to dance
and what's the music playing
                    Plutonium in your pants
Yeah the mass is crazed for energy
                    to fill our metal wants
and the capitalists are
                    angry at the communistic ants—

O I cant find anyone
                    to help me sing my song
to spread the Sacred Dharma
                    our suffering's been so long
my ignorance   my ego
                    keeps banging the angry gong
But I gotta find someone
                    Who's willing to be wrong
& stay on Earth & see the worth
                    of a road endlessly long

No I cant find anyone to talk to me with sense
I cant find anyone to cross the bony fence

I cant find anyone to work
                    the work's immense
It's the effort just to get here were we are
                    with common sense
The world of joy is empty, the real world is so dense—

I can't find anyone to show me what to do
I cant find anyone
                    It's maken me so blue
I cant find anyone
                    anyone but you
O I cant find anyone that knows me
                    good as you
Yeah I cant find anyone,
                    only you Guru

                    Dream April 24, 1975

GURU BLUES

Dream Stanza April 24, 1975

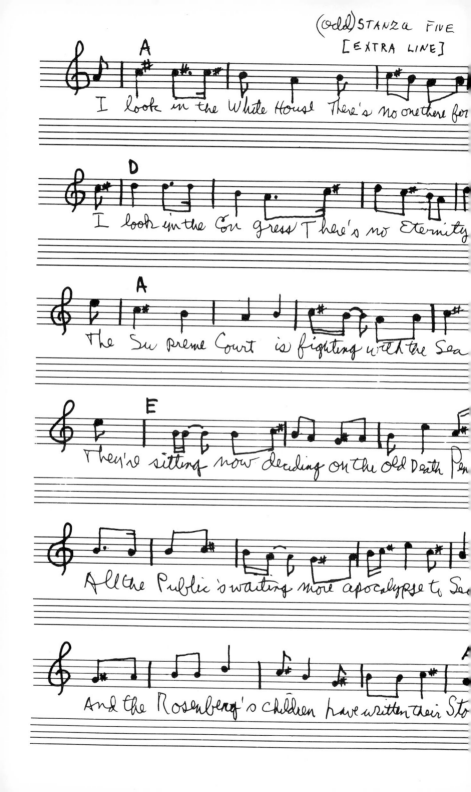

(odd) STANZA FIVE
[EXTRA LINE]

I look in the White House There's no one there for

I look in the Congress There's no Eternity

The Supreme Court is fighting with the Sea

They're sitting now deciding on the old Death Pen

All the Public's waiting more apocalypse to See

And the Rosenberg's children have written their Sto

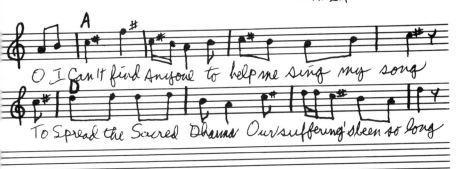

O I Can't find Anyone to help me sing my song

To spread the Sacred Dharma Our suffering's been so long

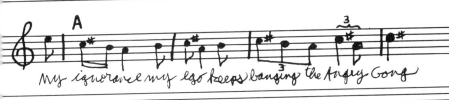

My ignorance my ego keeps banging the Angry Gong

But I Gotta find someone Who's willing to be wrong

& stay on Earth & see the Worth Of a Road that's endless long

RYTHMIC STEMS AND BARS BY GEORGE ROWE   JULY 4, 1975

Guru (Num-Dro) Blues Allen Ginsberg Boulder 30 June 1975

NAROPA INSTITUTE

CHORDS NOTEHEADS & BARLINES BY A.G.

THE AUTHOR

Allen Ginsberg, born in Newark, New Jersey in 1926, was raised in Paterson, New Jersey and attended Columbia University. He is the author of *Howl*, 1956, *Kaddish*, 1960, *Empty Mirror*, 1961, The *Yage Letters*, 1963, *Reality Sandwiches*, 1963, *Wichita Vortex Sutra*, 1967, *Planet News*, 1968, *T.V. Baby Poems*, 1968, and *Fall of America*, 1974.